THIS BOOK BELONGS TO

____